T0195964

Alphabet Soup for the Bored!

Oodles of Noodles to Doodle!

Jeri Lynn Piechoski

Archway Publishing books may be ordered through booksellers or by contacting:

Archway Publishing
1663 Liberty Drive
Bloomington, IN 47403
www.archwaypublishing.com
1 (888) 242-5904

ISBN: 978-1-4808-9078-7 (sc)
ISBN: 978-1-4808-9079-4 (e)

Print information available on the last page.

Archway Publishing rev. date: 05/15/2020

ABCDEF
GHIJKL
MNOPQR
STUVW
XYZ

A B C D E F

F G H I J K L

M N O P Q R

S T U V W

X Y Z

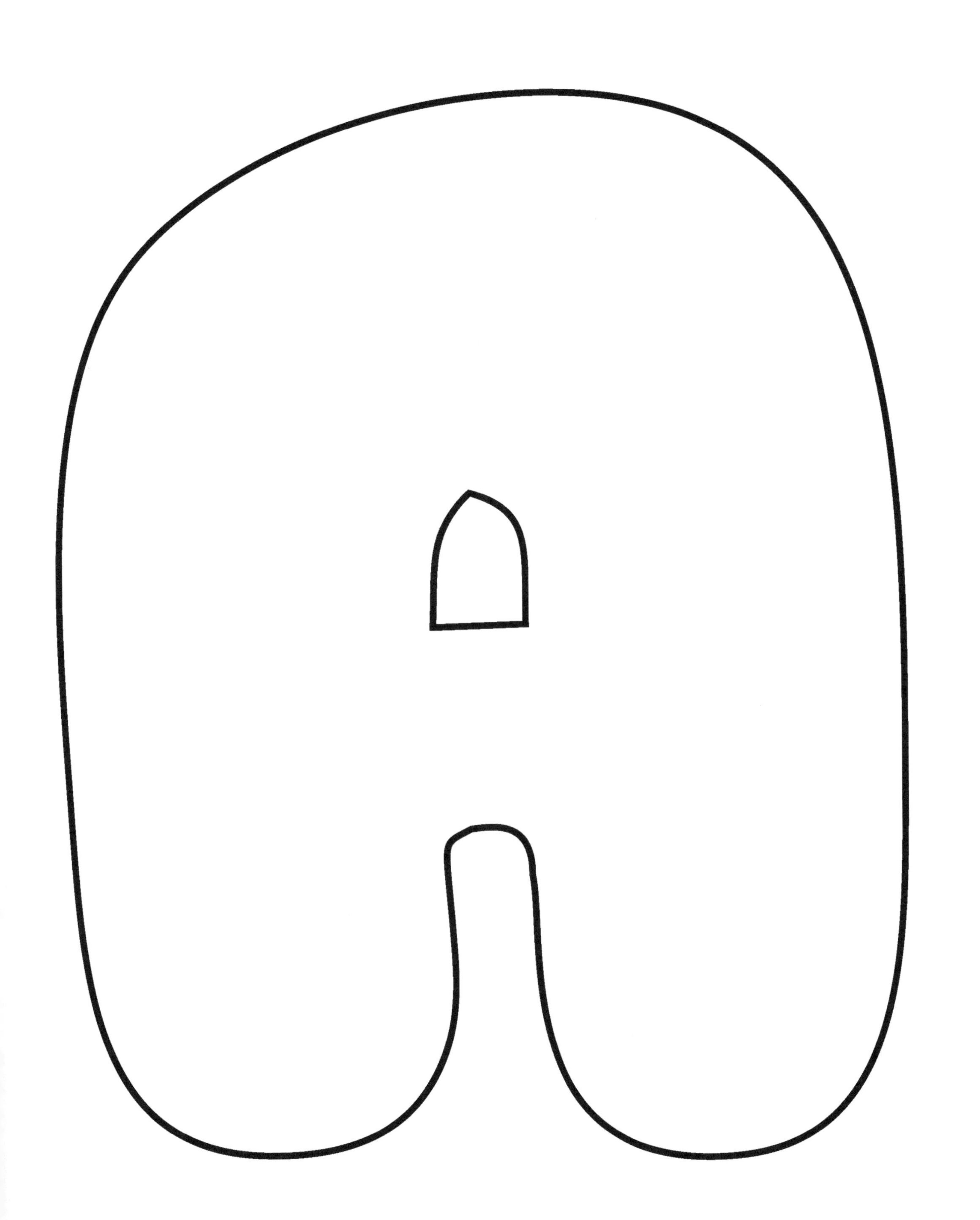

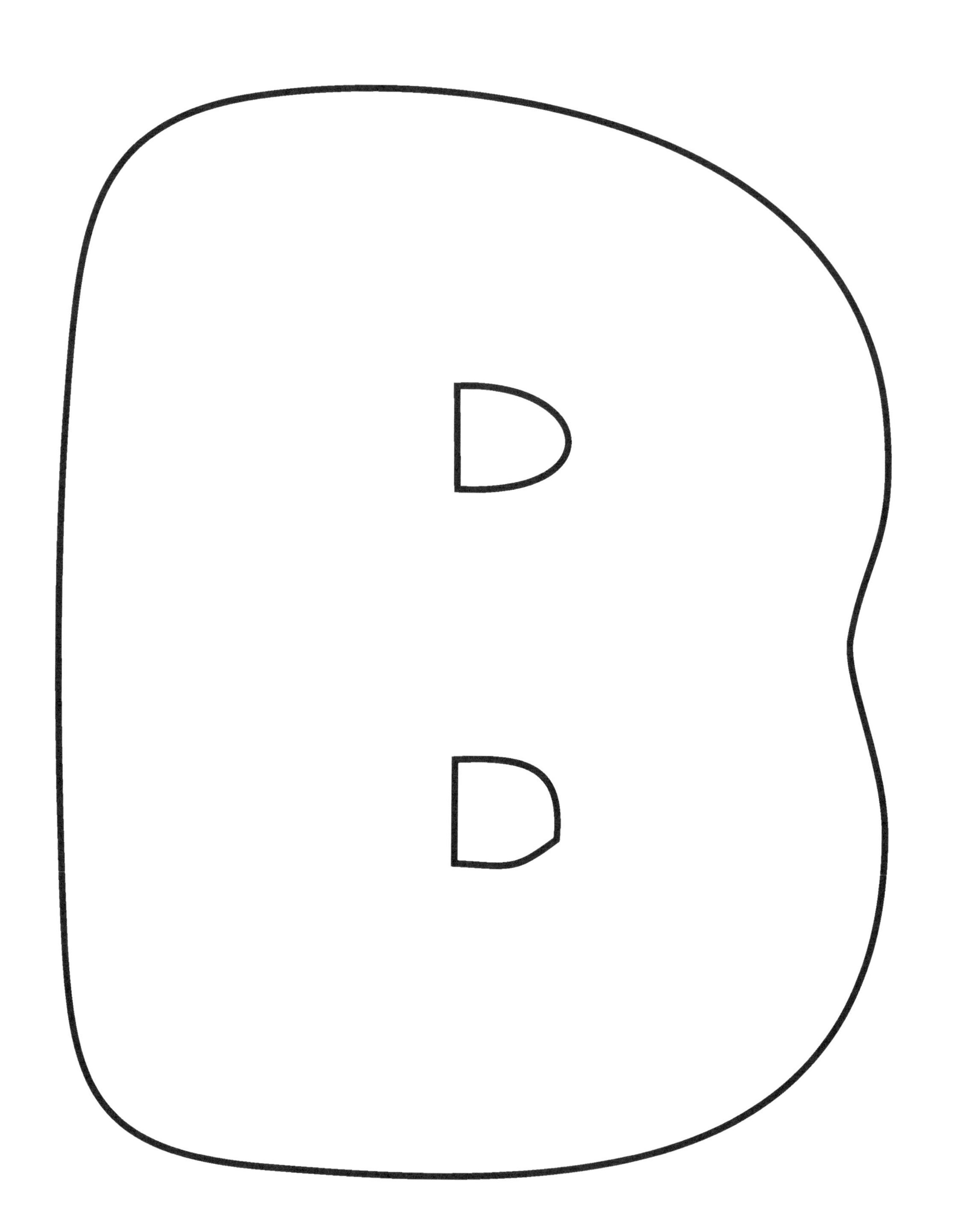

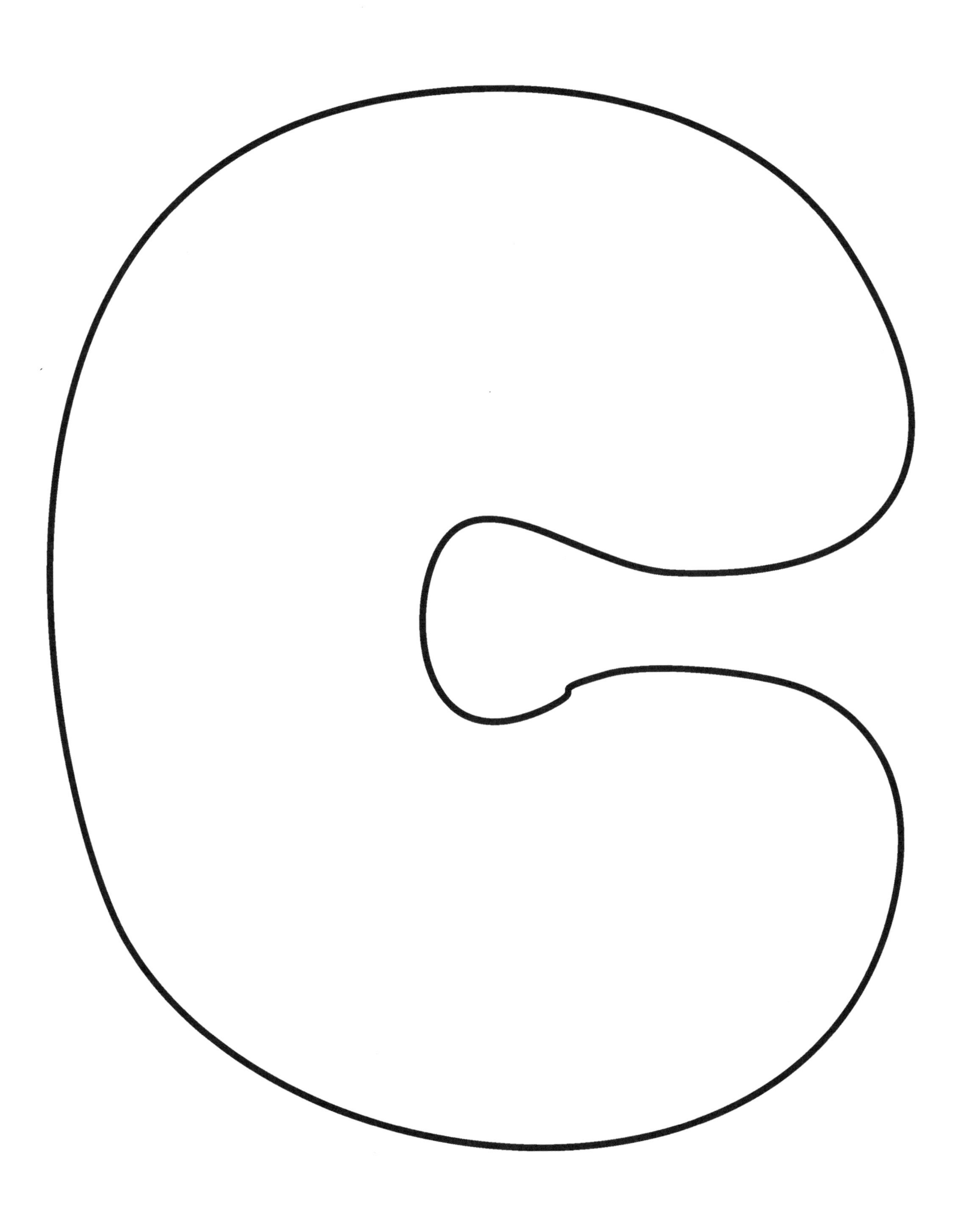

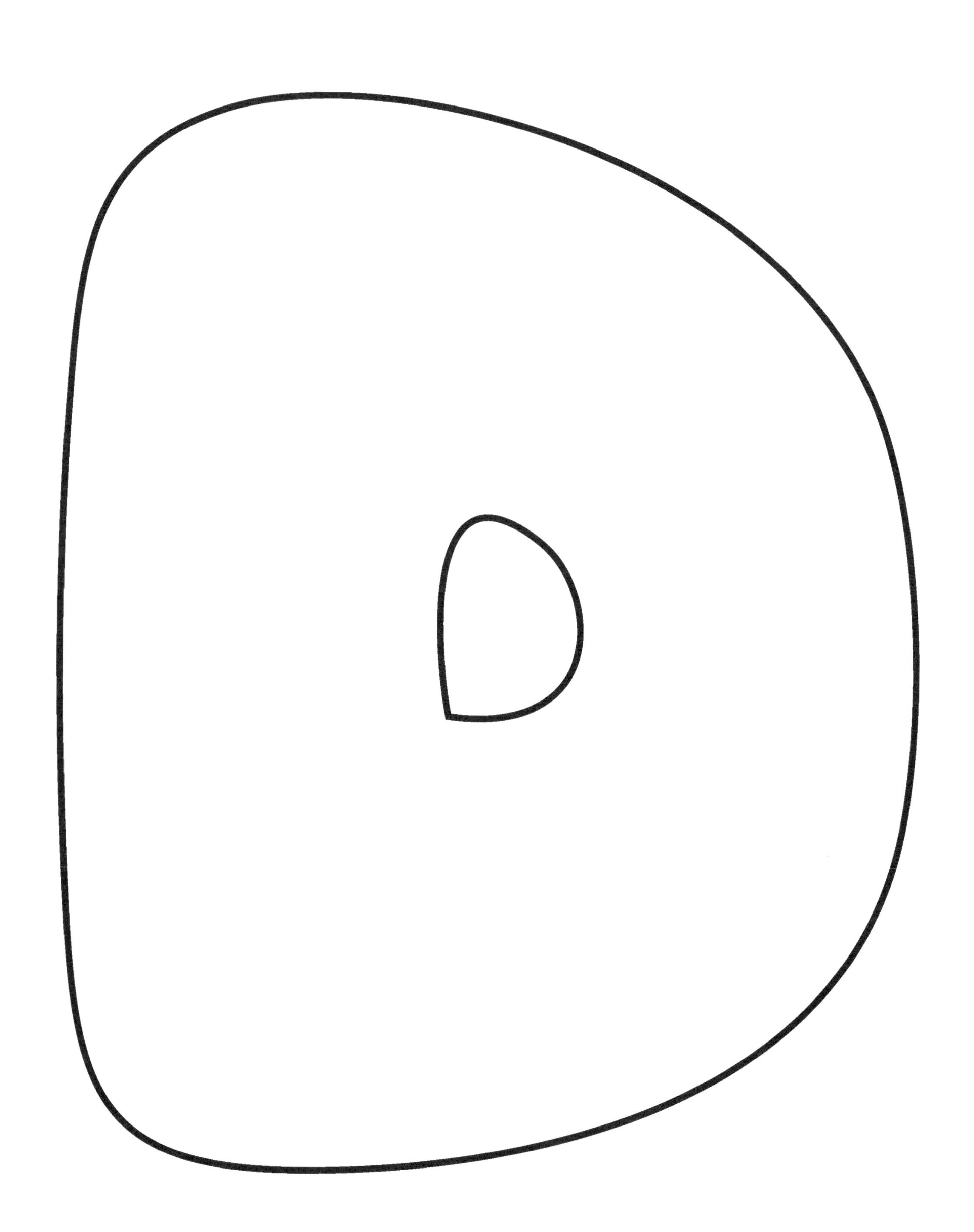

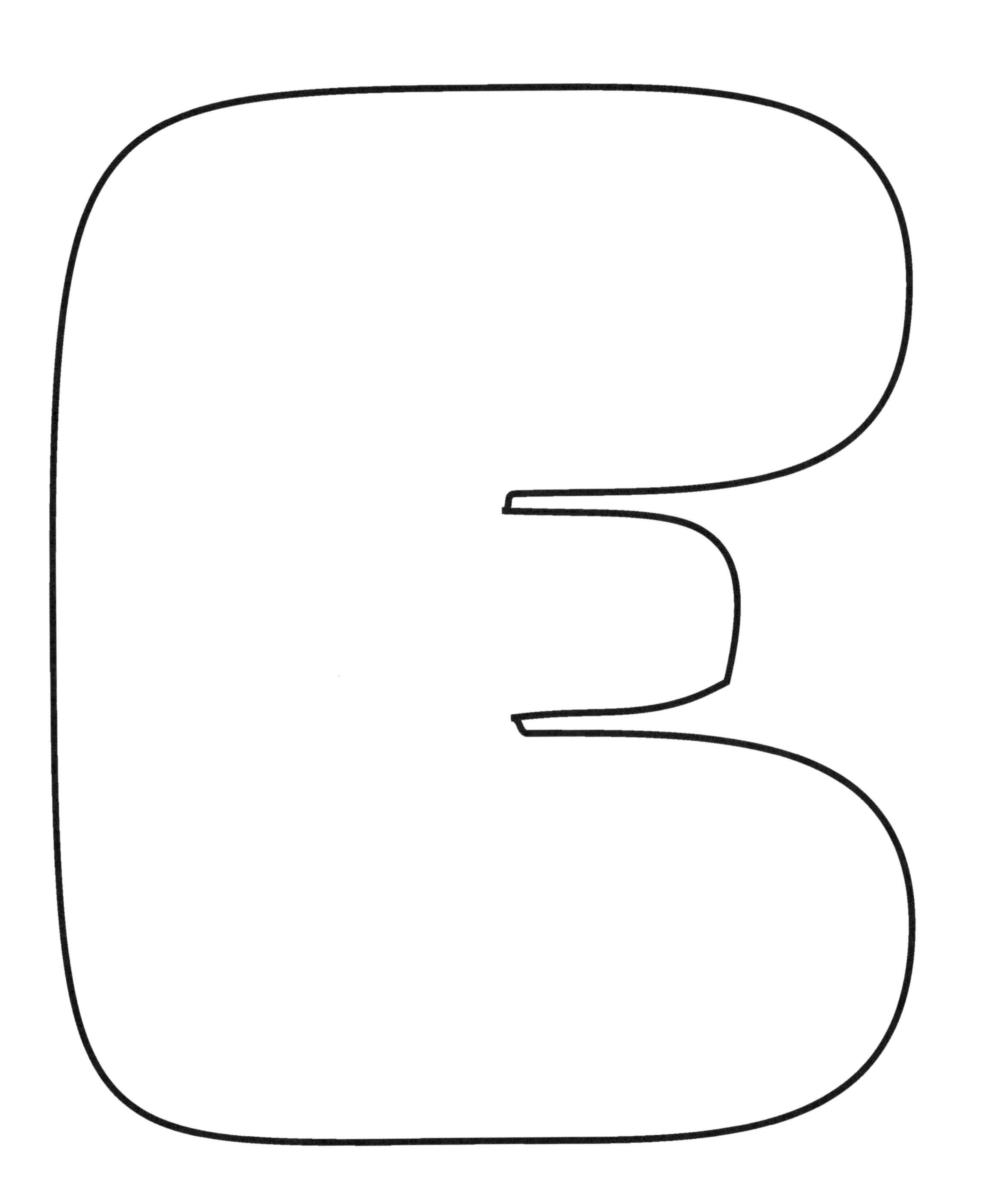

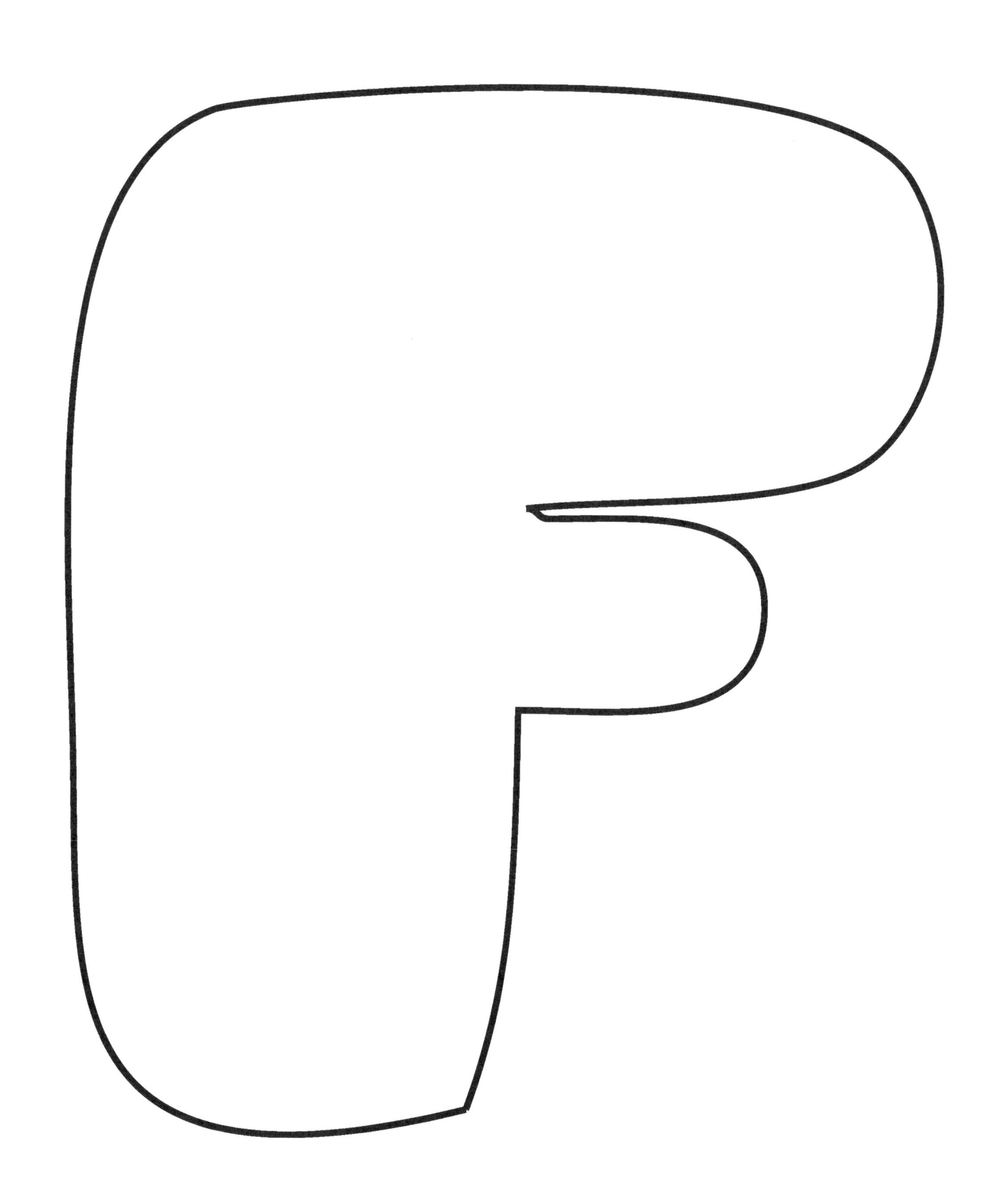

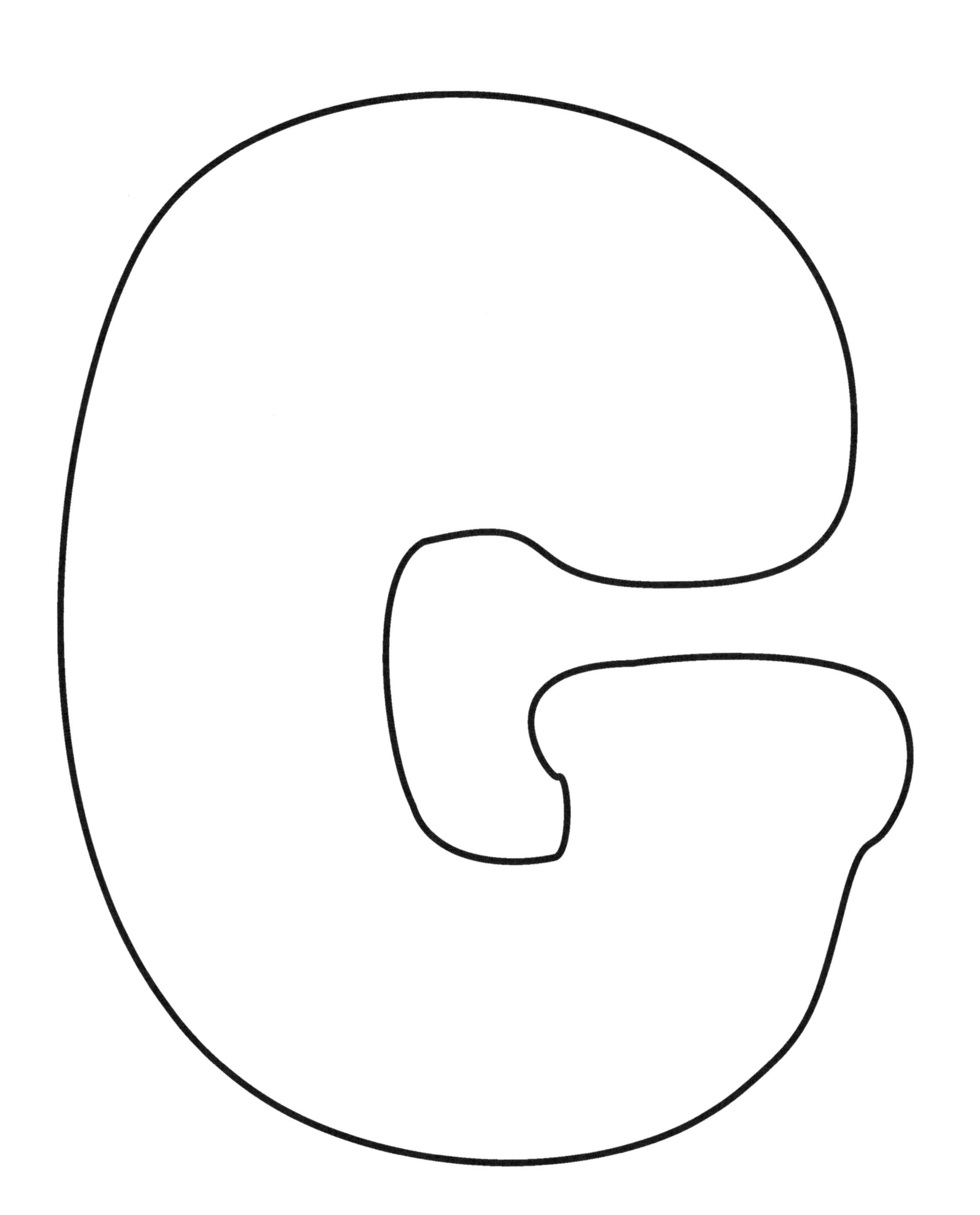

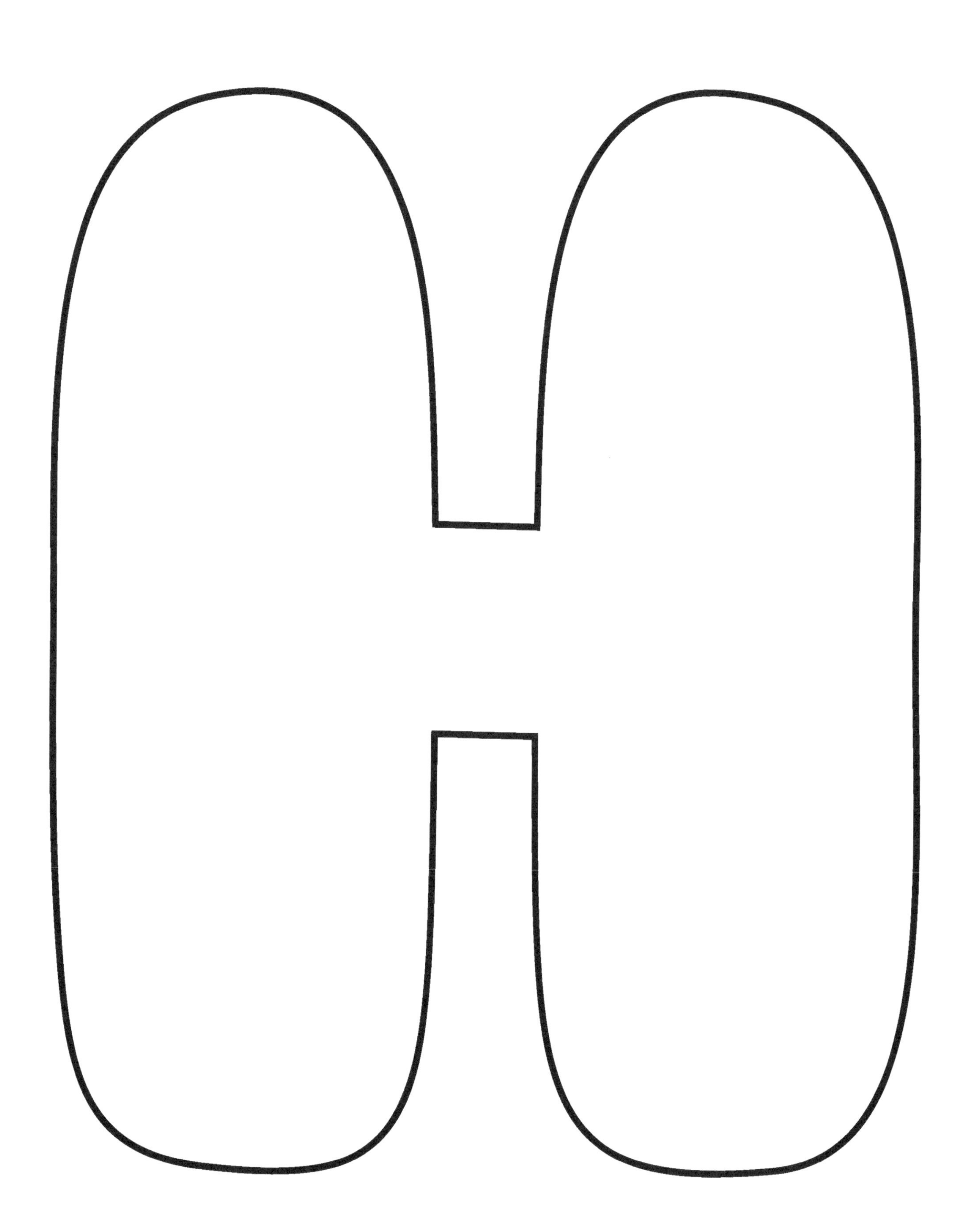

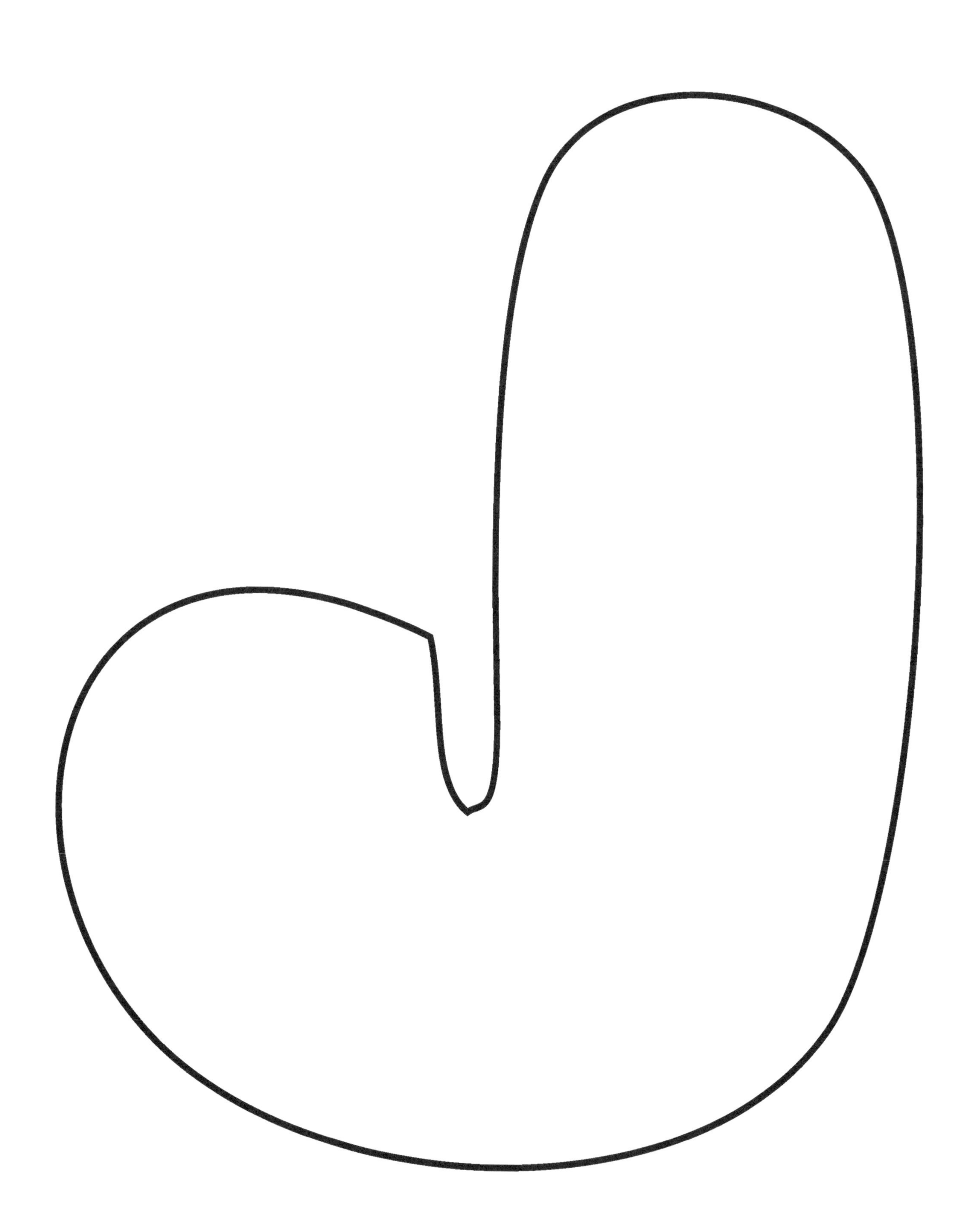

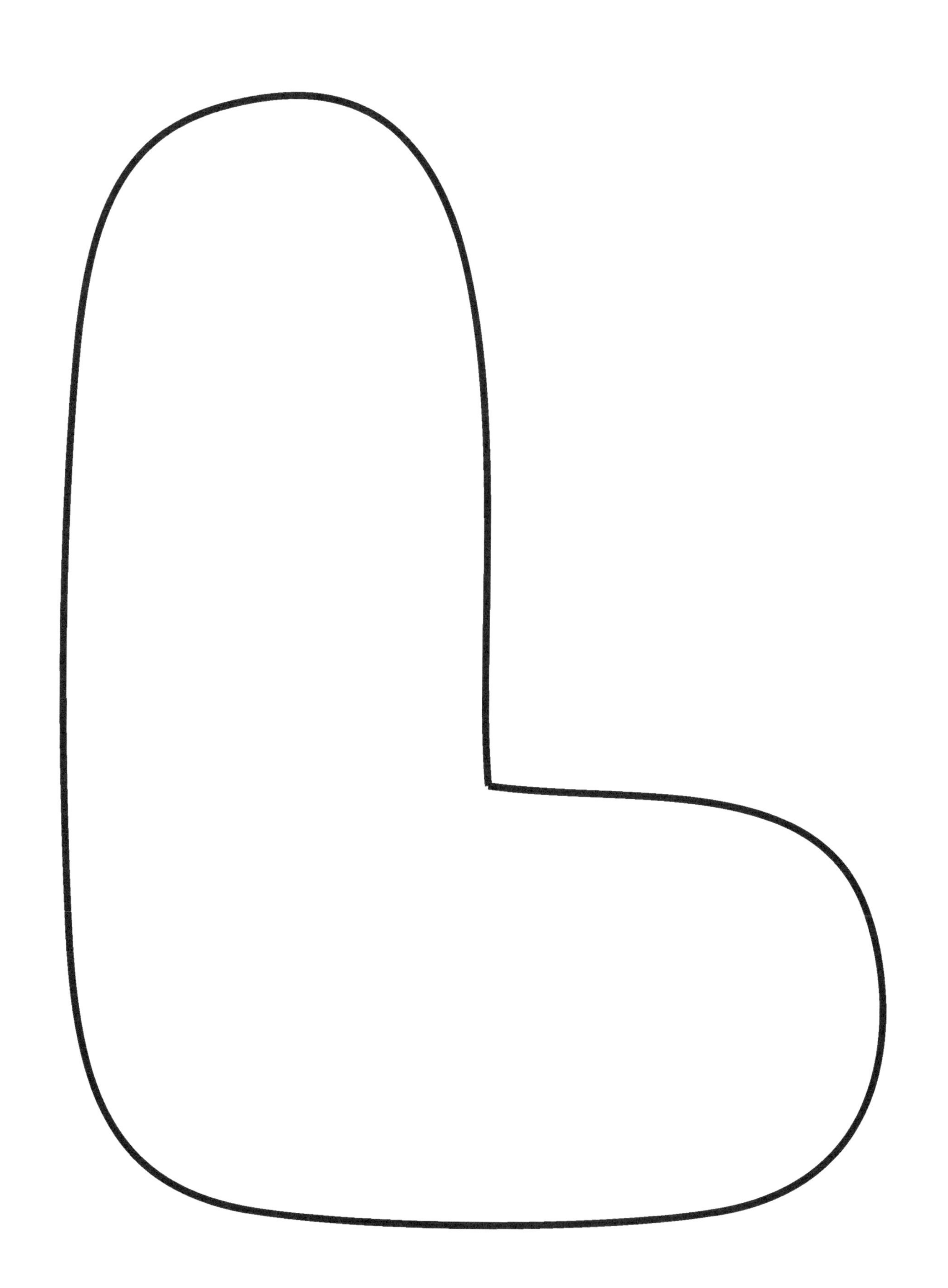

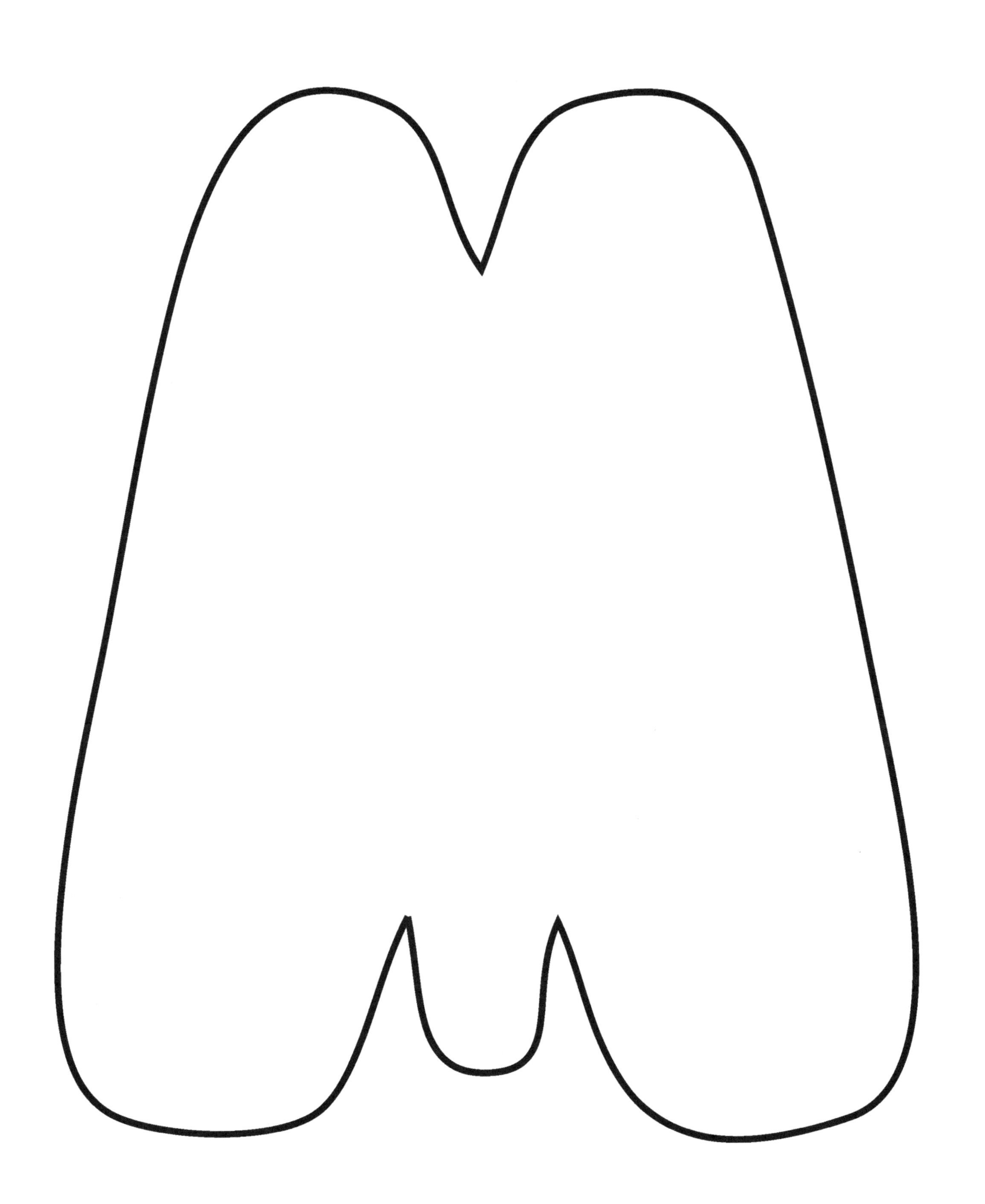

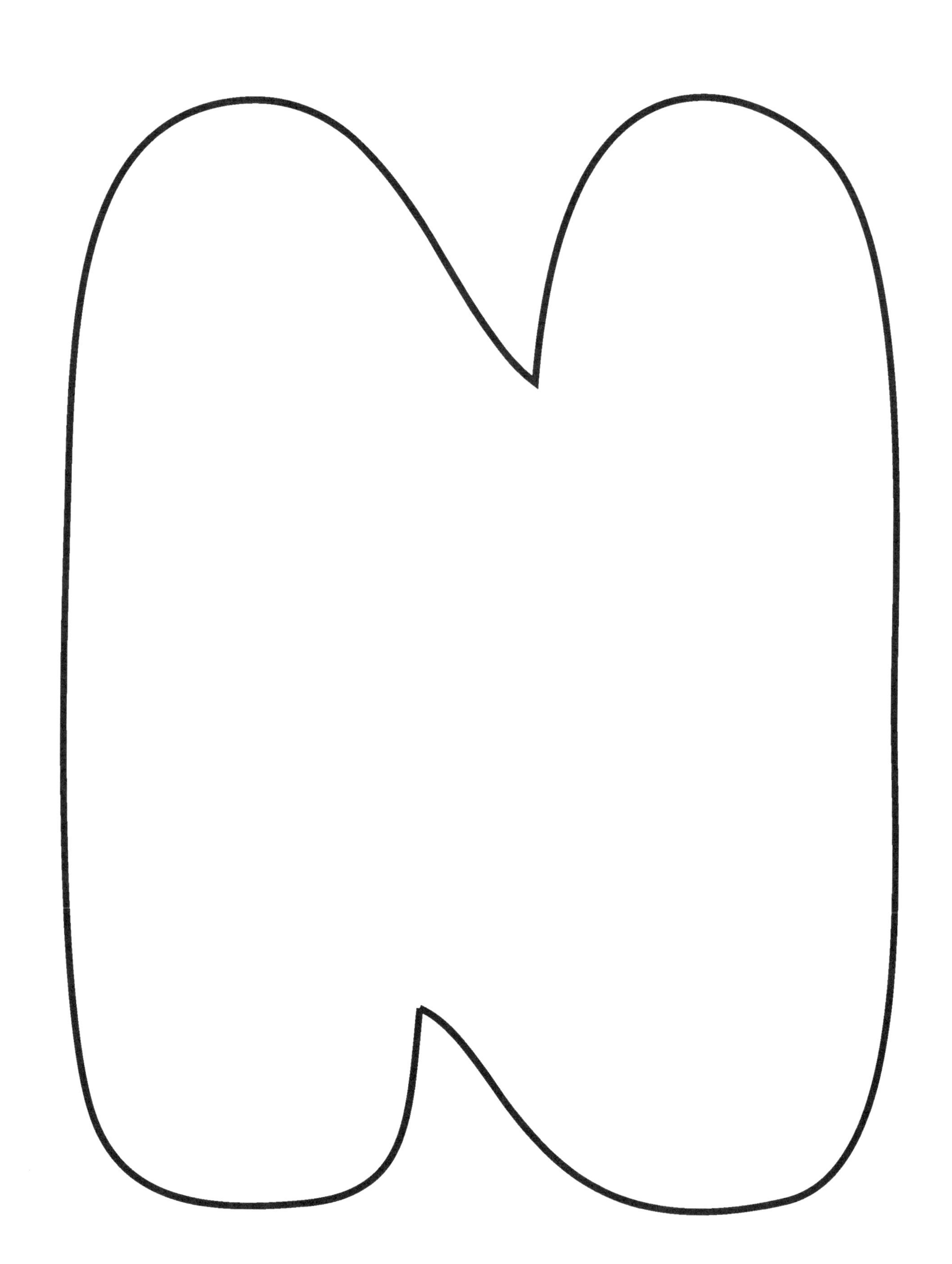

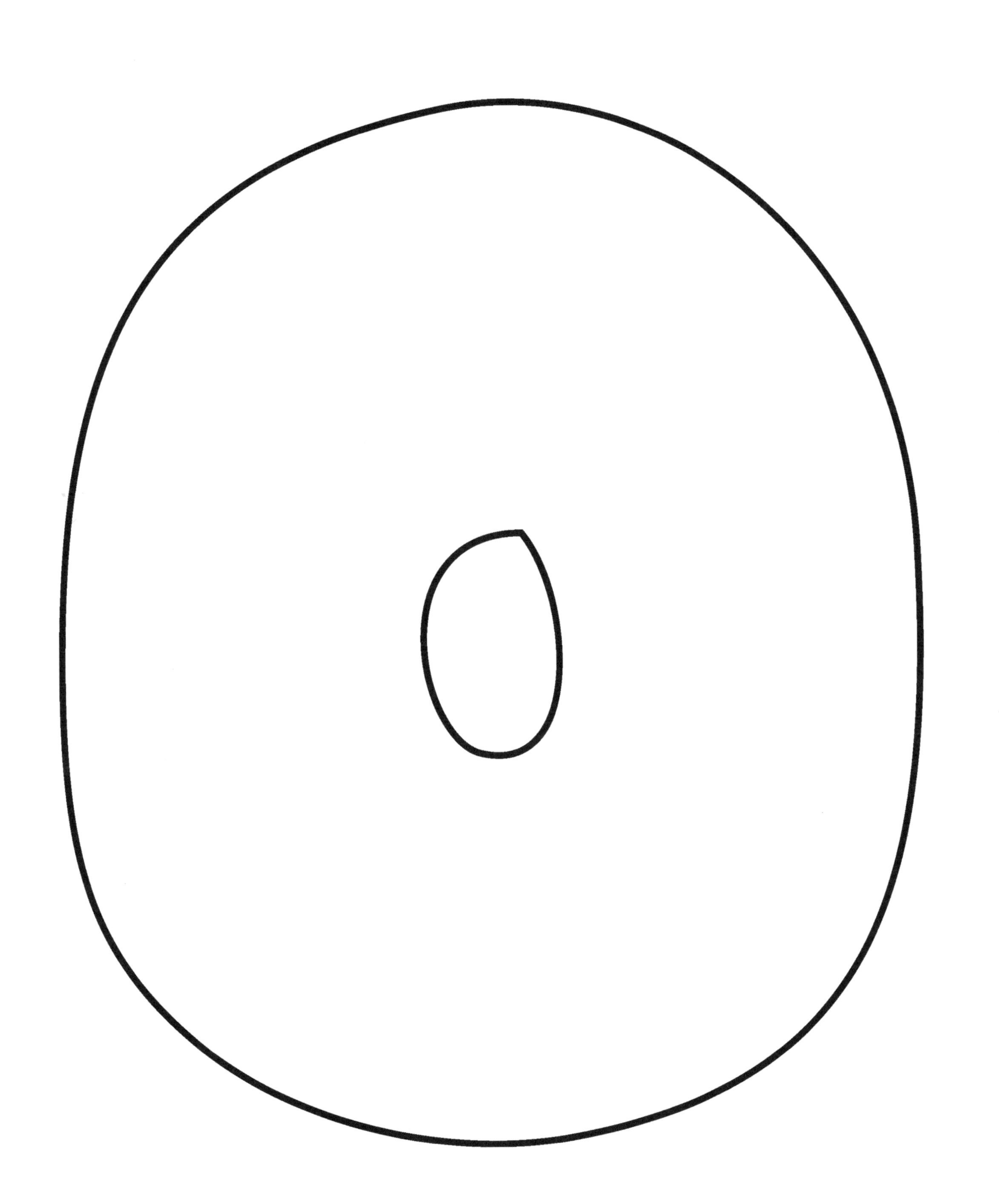

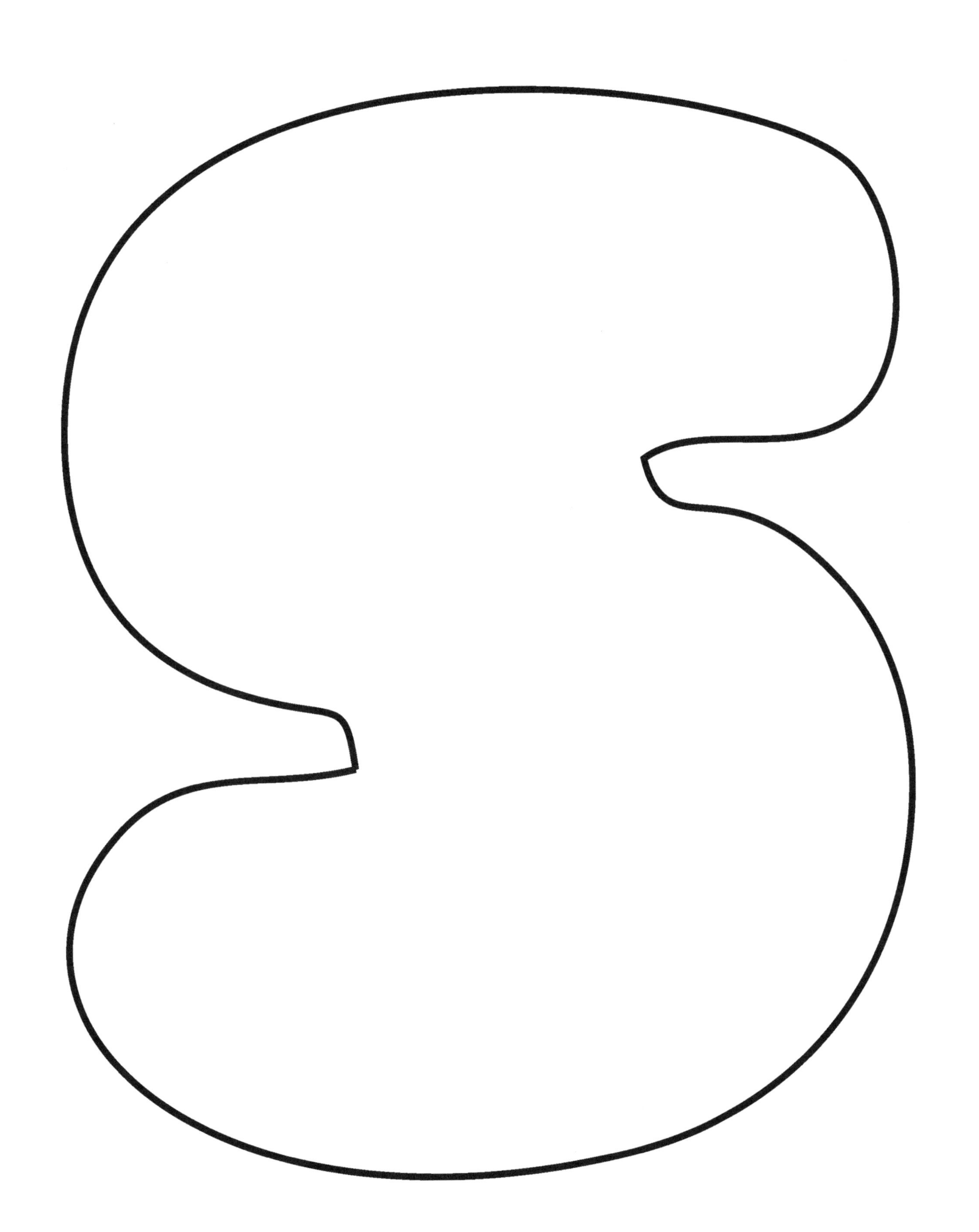

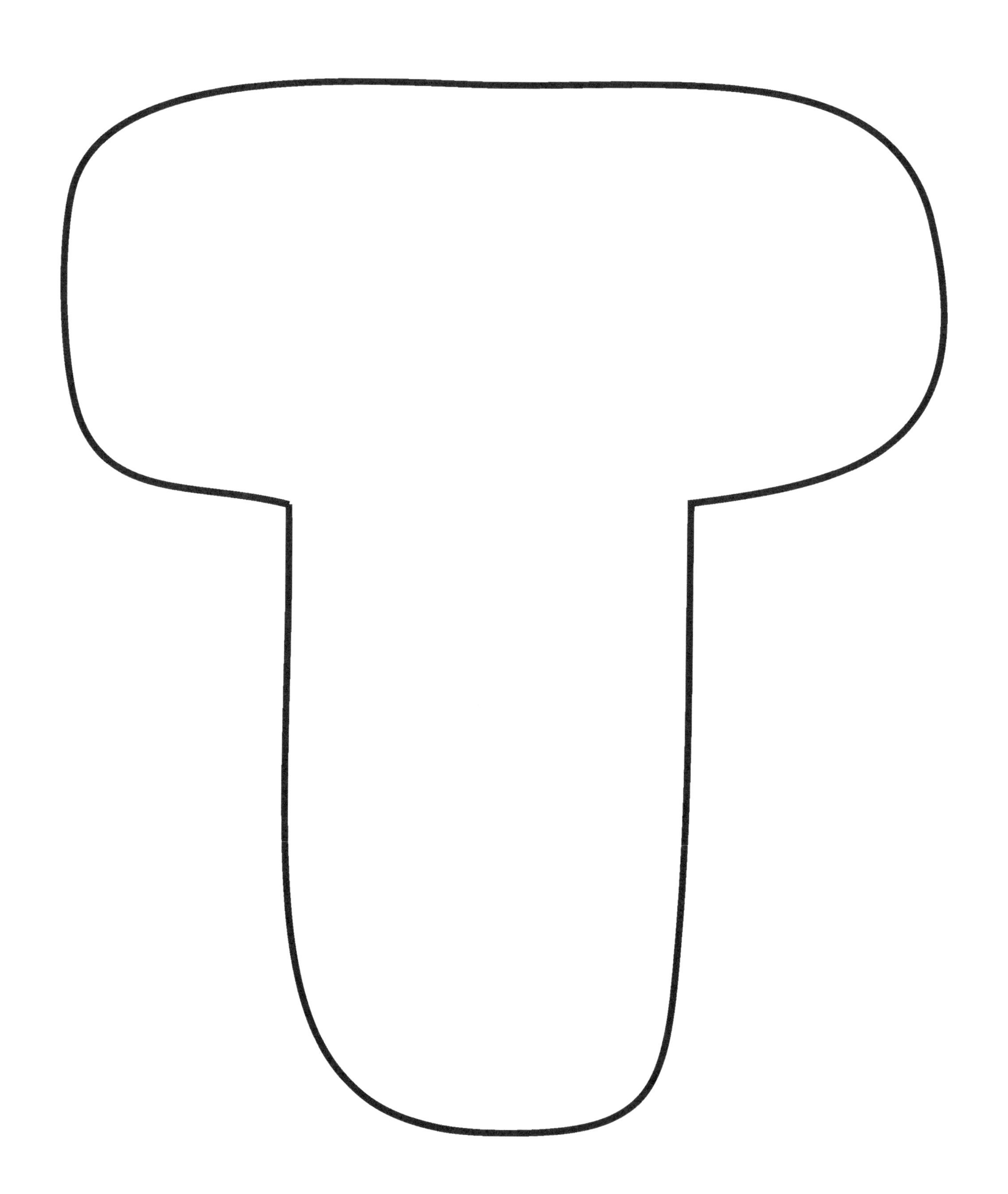

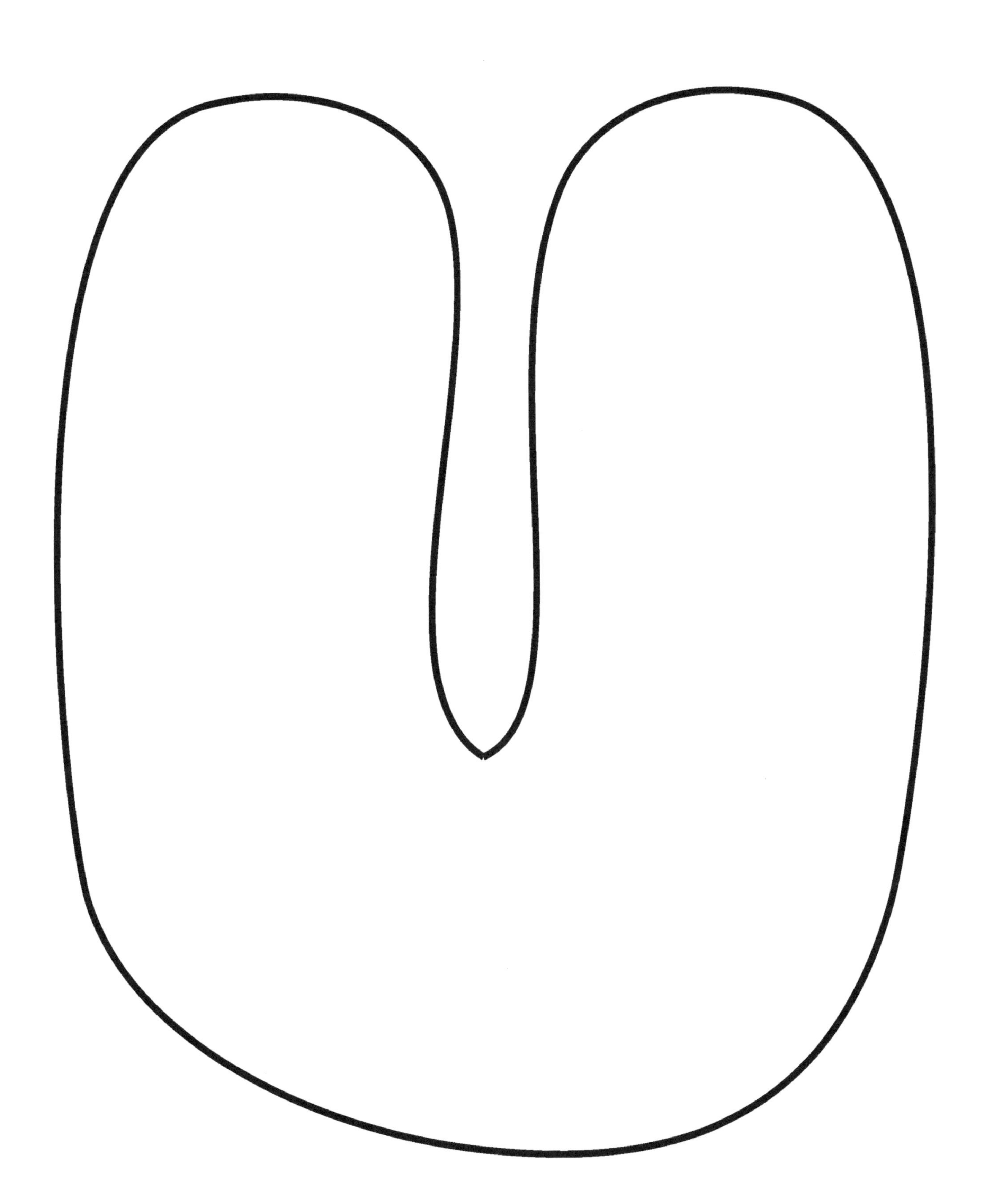

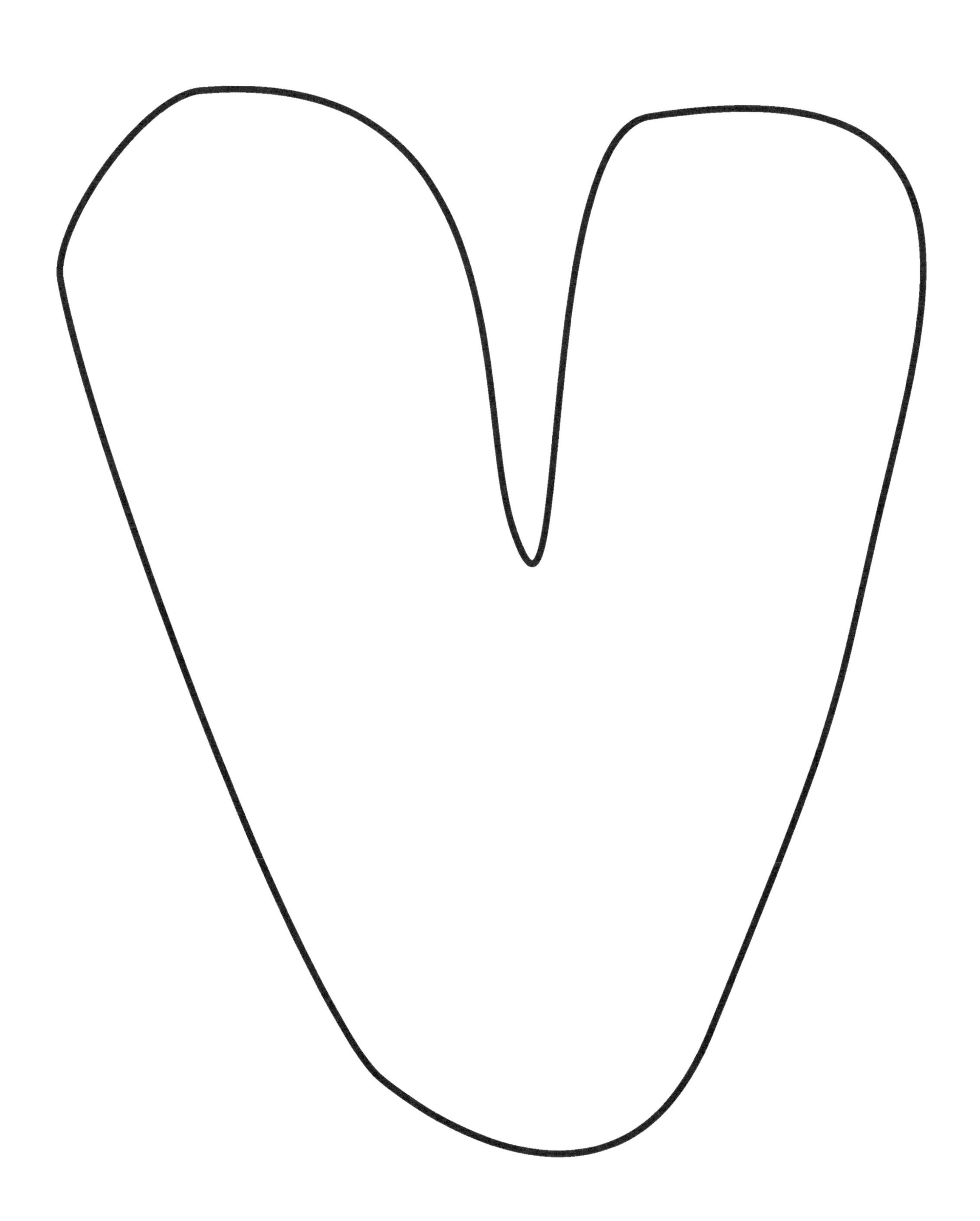

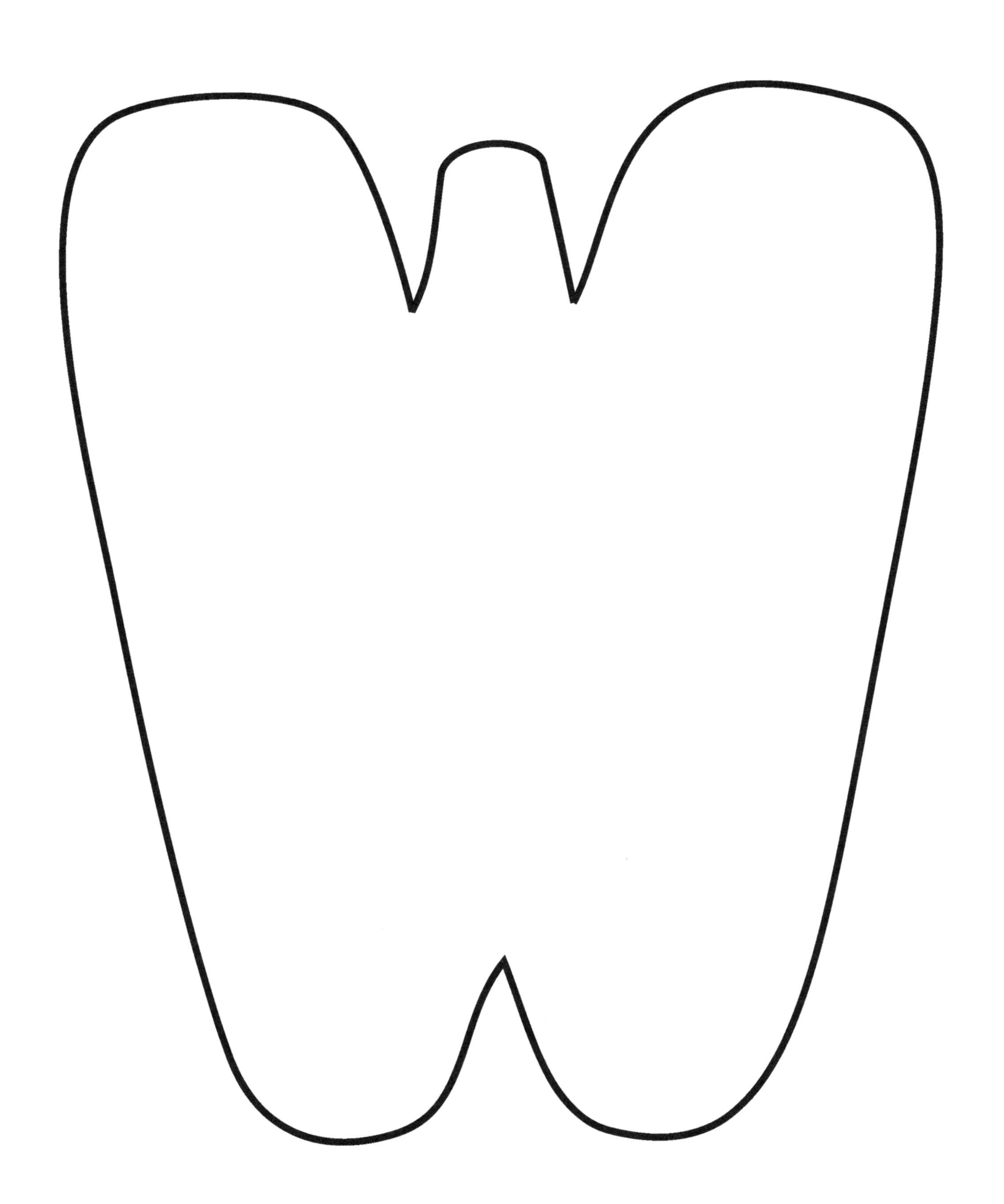

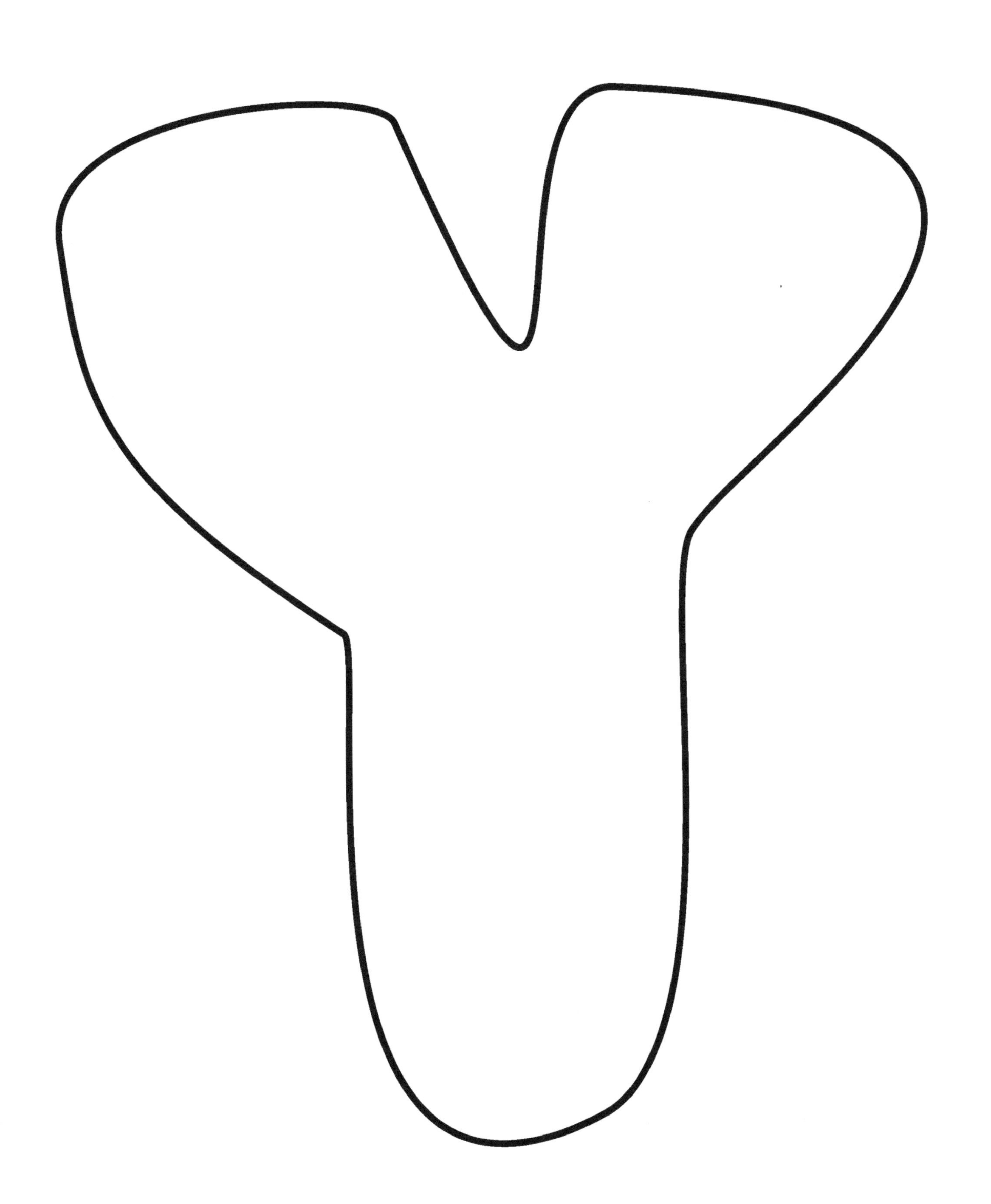

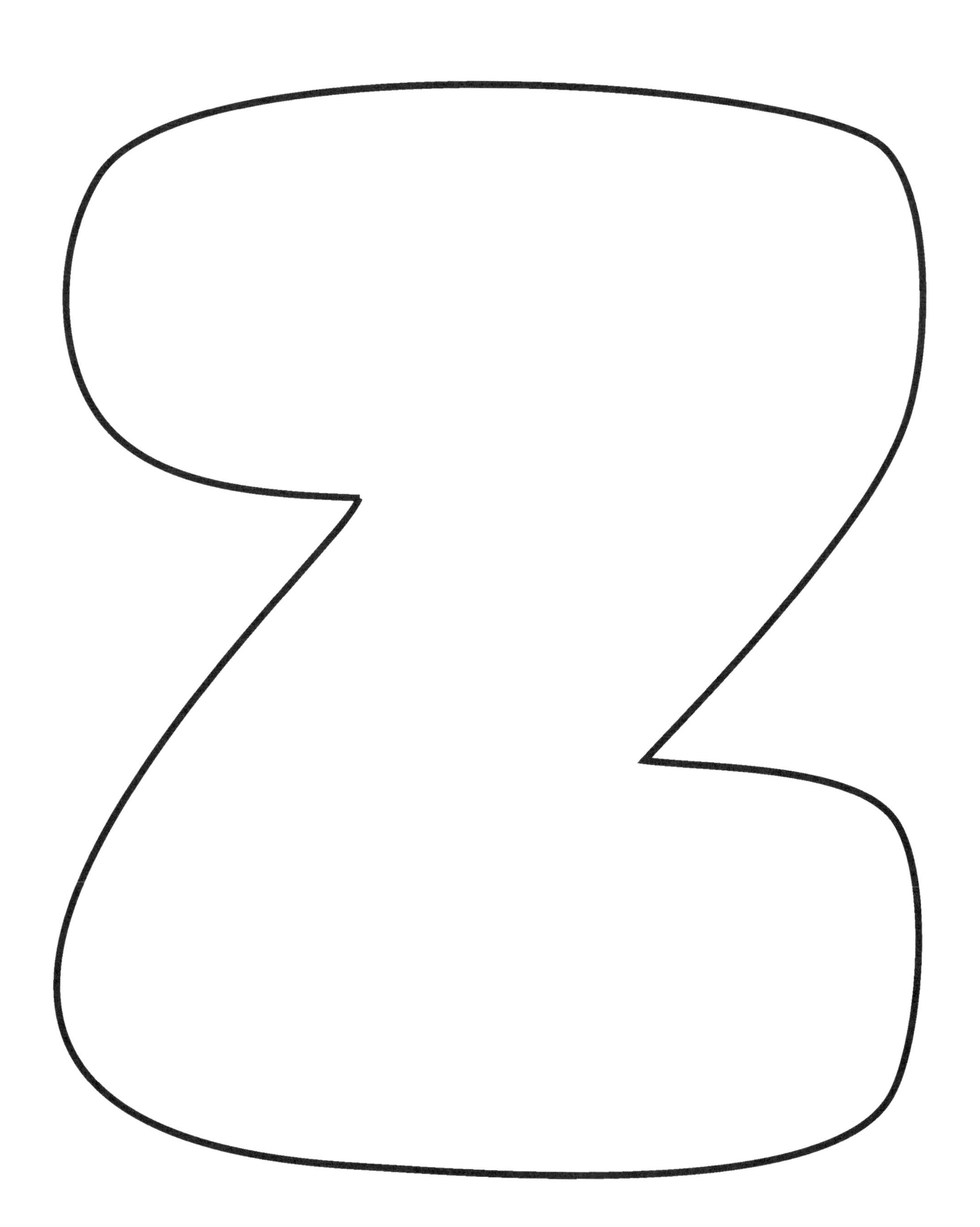

As an elementary school art teacher for seventeen years, **Jeri Lynn Piechoski**'s lesson plans were creative and punny. She always encouraged her students to think outside the box and the lines when it came to creating their "masterpieces." So when the adult coloring book craze began in 2015, she was inspired to create a new type of coloring book. She wanted one that had large open shapes (bubble alphabet letters, that is!) plus blank pages ready to be filled up with doodles, thoughts, words, lines, shapes, and designs by using any type of art medium. She even came up with a clever book title—*Alphabet Soup for the Bored*—a parody of the popular book series *Chicken Soup for the Soul*. Instead of 101 inspiring stories and essays to read, 26 letters would provide the open space for inspirational coloring and doodling.

Printed in the United States
By Bookmasters